PICK YOUR FLOWER POEM

by NancyLee

First Edition

ISBN: 9798986913124 - *Paperback*
ISBN: 9798986913131 - *eBook*

Contact Us
sheshexpressions@gmail.com

Printed in the United States of America

I would like to dedicate this book
to my grandchildren who are
always an inspiration in keeping
me young at heart.

I'll pick my flower
my flower to be is
a
a purple petunia
super tuff just like
me.

It's
large ruffled blooms like a
lost treasure
or a family heirloom
they are beautiful in sight
with
colorful delight
that would be me the petunia
that shows off
all that I thrive to be.

I'll pick my flower
my flower
to be is a sunflower
that's
shining like me.

yellow gold bright and bold
I too stand strong and tall
there is plenty of me that last
way past fall
so a sun flower it will be of course
that's only one half of me.

I"LL PICK MY FLOWER MY FLOWER TO BE IS A ROSE TALL AND BEAUTIFUL JUST LIKE ME.

MY SOFT SILKY PETALS
AND STRONG LONG
STEM MAKE ME
SEPARATE FROM THE
REST OF THEM.
YES I AM BEAUTIFUL
I AM BRIGHT
AND MAKE YOU SMILE
WHEN IN SIGHT.
SO A PINK ROSE IT
WILL BE THAT'S THE
FLOWER YOU WILL SEE
IN ME .

I'LL PICK MY FLOWER
MY FLOWER TO BE IS A
RED TULIP THAT
REPRESENT ME .

VIBRANTLY RED THE HEART
OF LOVE
THAT FITS ME PERFECT
LIKE A HAND TO A
GLOVE
SO A TULIP IT WILL BE
DEEP WITH TRUE LOVE
INSIDE OF ME,

SO PICK YOUR
FLOWER
AND TELL US NEXT
TIME

WHAT FLOWER IN
YOU WOULD COME
TO MIND.

ARE YOU
TALL
STRONG,
VIBRATE AND
LOVED JUST
TO MENTION
A FEW
THAT MAY
LIE WITHIN
YOU.

OR MAYBE
THERE'S A
SPECIAL FLOWER
YOU WOULD
WANT TO SHARE
THAT TELLS US
ALL ABOUT THE
KINDNESS THAT
YOUR FLOWER
BARE.

UNTIL WE SPEAK
AGAIN LETS ALL
SHOW OFF THE FLOWER
THAT WE ARE

to bring forth the
beauty

like a bright

shining star.